Gateway to America: New York City

Erik V. Krustrup

Gateway to America:
New York City

The Dream of America

ₜ **Creative Education**

The Dream of America

The series consists of

1 Europe and the Flight to America.
2 America Fever
3 The Westward Journey
4 They Came to America
5 Gateway to America: New York City
6 Shattered Dreams: Joe Hill
7 Ireland in Flight

Editor (Danish edition): Flemming Lundahl
Picture Editor: Anita Amundsen
Covers: Nancy Arend
English Edition translated and edited by J. R. Christianson & Birgitte Christianson
Cover photo: USIS

Danish Edition © 1976 by Munksgaard/Copenhagen
English Edition © 1982 by Creative Education, Inc.

Library of Congress Catalog Card No.: 81-71513
Author: Krustrup, Erik
        Gateway to America.
Mankato, MN: Creative Education, Inc.
72 P.
8201   811124
ISBN: 0-87191-709-2

Contents

First Impressions

The Statue of Liberty

Rain was pouring down in New York. Crowds of people were waiting along the docks.

The day had started out well. More than 100,000 guests had come to town during the morning. They had all come to see the great parade in the harbor.

Now everything was drowning in the rain. It was impossible to see what was happening out on the water of the harbor.

The day was Thursday, September 28, 1886. The newspapers called it Bartholdi Day.

The French sculptor, Frédéric-Auguste Bartholdi, was at this very moment on his way out to witness the unveiling of his life's greatest masterpiece: the Statue of Liberty. The statue stood on a little island, Bedloe's Island, at the mouth of New York harbor.

Three hundred beautifully decorated paddlewheel steamers lined both sides of the route. They were prepared to blow their steam whistles when the ship and its guests reached Bedloe's Island.

The Statue of Liberty used as an advertising symbol.

The boat with President Grover Cleveland and his party came last.

The French engineer, Ferdinand de Lesseps, was also present. He had built the Suez Canal in the 1860's.

The Statue of Liberty was a gift to America from the French peo-ple. It symbolized the cooperation between the two nations during the American Revolution.

The Statue of Liberty was originally supposed to have been unveiled on the Fourth of July in 1876—the centennial of the Declaration of Independence. But the work got started too late. Only the right arm of the statue had been ready at that time.

The statue is a symbol of the idea of freedom. It immediately became a symbol of American freedom.

The Statue of Liberty was the first thing that European immigrants saw when they sailed into New York harbor.

Fund Raising

The Statue of Liberty was paid for with money contributed by the people of France. The Americans paid for the base themselves. That may not sound like much, but it was. The base and foundation had to be 150 feet high, and it turned out to be very expensive.

7

The Statue of Liberty under construction.

Fund raising went slowly in America. People did not seem to find it very inspiring to contribute money for a foundation.

When the statue was finished, there was still not enough money to build the upper part of the base. So the statue had to be stored in Paris for about a year.

The famous American publisher, Joseph Pulitzer—himself an immigrant—helped to publicize the need to complete the base.

By 1885, enough money had been raised. A message was sent to Paris that the statue could now be shipped to America.

It consisted of a skeleton of iron bars, 150 feet high, with a winding stairway inside. The skeleton was covered with more than 300 specially formed copper plates. The whole statue was easy to take apart and put together again.

On June 19, 1885, the statue arrived in New York aboard the French ship, "Isère," in 214 boxes.

Dedication

Bartholdi was cheered like a king on the day of the dedication. Twenty thousand soldiers marched down Fifth Avenue in his honor. Military bands played and people sang the "Marseillaise" and "Yankee Doodle."

Fireworks for the dedication of the Statue of Liberty in 1886. In the foreground, a section of the New York harbor area.

9

But the afternoon festivities were something of a fiasco because of the rain.

One of New York's popular weeklies, *Frank Leslie's Illustrated Newspaper,* reported as follows:

November 6, 1886

Soldiers lined the battlements, and over 2,000 persons were upon the grand stand. Very few ladies were present, on account of the bad weather. The President sat in the middle of the covered platform, with Bartholdi on his right and Count de Lesseps on his left.

The exercises began about 3:15, amidst a pandemonium of artillery salutes from the war-ships, and shrieks from hundreds of steam whistles above which were heard at intervals the strains of French and American national airs. A floating city of ships surrounded the island. The tars manned the yards, and bunting was flung out lavishly. Over all drifted the clouds of mist, steam and gunpowder smoke, giving a perculiarly weird aspect to the wonderful picture.

The First Skyscrapers

The Statue of Liberty was the tallest structure in New York for the next twenty years, followed by the spire of Trinity Church and the towers of the Brooklyn Bridge. All three structures were around 300 feet high.

The Statue of Liberty was a breathtaking sight for the hundreds of thousands of immigrants who sailed right past it on their

trance to New York harbor, where the waters were filled with ships. The returning Americans searched for the Statue of Liberty, which to them is the symbol of the wonderful, free land of America. But my eyes were drawn to some high,

way to the immigration station at Castle Garden.

It was not many years, however, before the buildings on land began to draw as much attention as the statue.

Holger Begstrup wrote in his book, *My Trip to America,* in 1925, "On Friday we saw the coast of Long Island with its glittering summer homes and hotels along the beach. We soon neared the encloud-like structures further inland. These were the skyscrapers of Manhattan.

"When we came nearer to these proud giants, I was so struck by the dramatic and wonderful sight that I almost forgot to look at the Statue of Liberty in our wake.

"Yes, these great buildings that stood together in a mass, with the high tower of the Woolworth Building reaching above the others—that was a sight I shall never forget. It was the greeting of a new and powerful country, bearing witness to the power and ingenuity of human beings.

"The skyscrapers are not simply huge. They are wonderfully beautiful. I was reminded of immense cactus plants."

The Hudson River in 1897. New York is beginning to become a city of skyscrapers.

Impressive Buildings

Skyscrapers began to become a part of New York's skyline around 1900. The first skyscraper was built in 1890. This was Joseph Pulitzer's 18 story headquarters building for his newspaper, the New York *World*.

In 1902, the narrow, 21 story Fuller Building on the corner of Broadway and Fifth Avenue was built. Because of the building's pointed, triangular shape, it came to be called the "flat iron."

In 1913, the American architect, Cass Gilbert, broke all records with his Woolworth Building, 800 feet high and the world's tallest building at that time.

No wonder the artists and writers of the world were fascinated. One of them, the Danish winner of the Nobel Prize for literature, Johannes V. Jensen, wrote about the architecture of New York in 1929. Of the "flat iron" building he wrote, "It is a matchless product of the pointed, triangular lot on which it was built and which determined its crazy shape. The dizzying height is due to the fact that the high value of the land forced it to shoot into the air.

One of New York's early skyscrapers, the Fuller Building.

12

"If one looks at details, it is horrible. Ugly plaster frills are everywhere. But the total impression is stylish—an elementary architectural power has left its mark.

"However, shame on questionable criticism as long as New York is as it is, unfinished, growing madly, indomitable and wonderful."

Before the Skyscrapers

New York was also able to impress strangers before it ever had skyscrapers.

The spire of Trinity Church was still the symbol of the city in 1872. A writer described the traffic in New York harbor at that time: "The short ferry ride from New York to Brooklyn gives a wide view of the enormous traffic in New York harbor.

"There are plans to connect New York and Brooklyn with a gigantic bridge that will begin far inside the two cities and go over streets and houses and be suspended over the wide river between two giant towers.

New York's architectural history in one picture. In the foreground, the old City Hall, built 1812. Behind it, the 60 story Woolworth Building, built 1913. And behind that, the twin towers of the 110 story World Trade Center, built 1973.

Ferry between Manhattan and Brooklyn, 1898.

"The towers are already under construction, and many years will pass before the work is finished. But until then, traffic is still going back and forth on the famous New York ferries. They are large paddlewheel steamers that cross back and forth across the harbor, day and night.

"Vehicles are parked in the middle of the ferry in two long rows, and the wagons are crowded close together in the rush hours, working wagons and elegant coaches side by side.

"The two walkways on either side are for passengers. There are benches along the walls of the cabins. One cabin is for gentlemen, the other for ladies.

"The only difference is that no smoking is allowed on the women's side, and it is a bit more clean."

History, Harbor and Trade

Origins

Ships and trade created the city of New York. This creation was both quick and hectic.

The history of the city begins in 1624. In that year, Dutch colonists landed on Manhattan. They founded the colony of New Netherland.

Two years later, Peter Minuit, Director General of the Dutch West India Company, arrived to be governor of the colony. He immediately made contact with the local Native Americans. They exchanged gifts, and the meeting went well. A few days later, Minuit acquired permission for the Dutch to settle on Manhattan. In return, he gave gifts worth about $24.

A few houses and a fort were built on Manhattan. The town got along by farming and fur trading. When Governor Peter Stuyvesant took over in 1647, he boosted trade, built better docks, and improved the harbor.

But in 1664, four English frigates landed on Manhattan. The

city surrendered to English armed force without a fight. The English took over and gave the colony a new name: New York. The Dutch governor was replaced by an English governor. Otherwise, life went on as usual.

In 1673, the Dutch re-conquered the city. It was now renamed New Orange. Otherwise, there were not many changes.

Just one year later, the English reconquered the city, and it became New York again. Then there was peace for about 100 years.

The Declaration of Independence in 1776 led the English to increase the number of soldiers they had in New York. Several bloody battles of the American Revolution were fought in the New York area. The English did not finally leave the city until 1783.

New York was the capital of the United States of America from 1785 to 1790. President George Washington and the government were in New York. Then in 1790,

Drawing of New York around 1660. It looks like a small Dutch city.

the capital was moved for a time to Philadelphia.

After that, the city of New York turned to trade. It had a tremendous potential in that area.

Harbor

A good harbor is necessary for a city that wants to be a center of trade. This was especially true in the days before highways, railroads and airplanes.

Governor Stuyvesant realized this in 1650, when he built the first little wharf in the East River. By 1750, 60 wharves had been built in the East River. Almost as many had been built on the other side of Manhattan in the Hudson River.

The Hudson wharves were not fully used until the 1850's, however. At that time, Cunard Line opened its docking facilities along the New Jersey side of the Hudson. The big Cunard passenger steamers from Europe docked there.

Many of these wharves were built and paid for by New York City. They were leased by auction.

Those who leased the wharves did not need to use them themselves. They could sell docking space to ships that wanted to enter the harbor. The only restriction was that the price could not exceed the top level set by the city council.

The rent in 1850 was very low. It was about ten times cheaper for a ship to unload in New York than in Boston or Baltimore. It was even cheaper compared to New Orleans or Charleston.

The cheap dock rental gave New York harbor a good reputation.

One other thing helped to make New York a major port city. It went back to the years around the end of the War of 1812 with England. At that time, English textile exporters decided to send all textiles to America by way of New York.

This meant that the rate of expansion of the port and harbor was stepped up tremendously.

Large supplies of textiles had accumulated in England during the war. At the same time, a great demand for textiles had grown up in America.

When peace came in 1814, England started to dump textiles on the American market. Ships were lined up to dock in New York harbor.

Export Harbor

It was not by coincidence that England chose New York as port of call for the textile trade in 1814.

The location was closer to Europe than most American harbors. New York was growing rapidly into the most important port on the east coast.

New York seen from the Hudson River, 1757.

18

New York harbor, 1878. The bowsprits of ships reach in over the busy street along the wharf.

In the space of ten years, New York had come to control almost the total American export of cotton. This was close to half of America's total export at that time.

All of these things were important to the growth of New York.

How could this happen? How could a northern harbor come to dominate the trade in cotton, a product grown in the South?

The answer is simple: it took a lot of nerve!

People in the South could not imagine that anyone would want to ship cotton all the way to New York before it was shipped to England. Anyway, they were more concerned with the problems of slavery and of growing the cotton than they were with shipping. At first, they hardly noticed that shipping agents from New York were

turning up throughout the South in the years around 1800. When they finally realized what was happening, it was too late. The cotton trade had been won away from the South, never to return.

The agents had "sneaked in the back door." But they also had lots of money behind them. They made good offers on freight, giving special discounts, extended credit and cheap loans. All they wanted

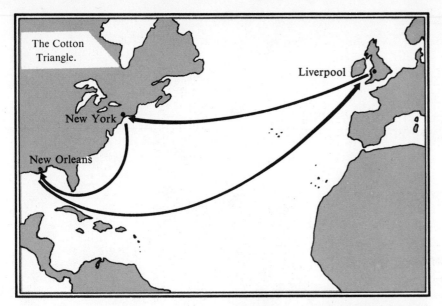

The Cotton Triangle.

like a triangle. The trip went, for example, from New Orleans to Liverpool to New York and back to New Orleans.

After 1815, the southern ports were gradually cut out of the triangle. Cotton was sent to New York. From New York, it was sent overseas. This was cheaper. The result was that New York grew big at the expense of other port cities on the Atlantic seaboard.

The Erie Canal

New York's leading position as an American port city was guaranteed when the Erie Canal was opened in 1825.

The canal connected Lake Erie with the Hudson River. It ran from Albany to Buffalo, New York.

New York City was already the port city for the whole eastern coast. Now it became the port city for the Midwest as well.

in return from the cotton growers was the right to sell the cotton overseas.

Big money could be earned by shipping cotton. There were profits for the agent, and also for the companies they represented.

Earlier, some ships had carried cotton directly from southern ports to Europe. They returned with goods of various kinds.

Sometimes ships sailed back from Europe by way of New York, carrying immigrants or freight. Then they had to sail empty from New York to their southern port. That was an extra expense for the ship owners.

This system was called the Cotton Triangle. The routes looked

Cotton mill around 1840. This machine prints a pattern on cotton cloth.

20

Digging the Erie Canal.

21

The Streets of New York

Broadway, September 28, 1886

The flags were drooping in heavy rain. The dedication of the Statue of Liberty was over. Broadway was returning to everyday life. Here and there, a street sweeper was pushing the debris of the celebration into the gutter.

It was hard to make much headway down the street because there were so many horse drawn carriages and wagons. The traffic moved slowly through the crowded streets. The drivers of the horse drawn omnibuses had to take advantage of every opening in the traffic in order to keep on schedule. Pedestrians had to move carefully when they tried to cross the street.

An Irish policeman pushed his way through the crowd of carriages, horses and human beings. Driving rules were unknown to most New Yorkers in those days. Automobiles did not exist yet.

New York street scene, 1883. Electric street lights had just been installed. Thomas Edison built New York's first electric plant in 1882.

Broadway (left) and Fifth Avenue intersect at Madison Square. This is where the "flat iron" building was built later.

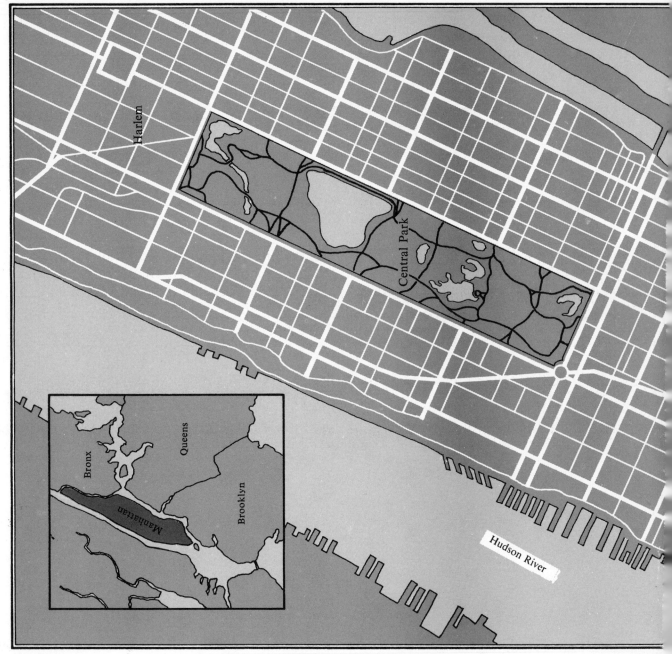

Harlem

Central Park

Hudson River

Bronx

Queens

Manhattan

Brooklyn

24

United Nations

Williamsburg Bridge

Lower East Side

Manhattan Bridge

Brooklyn Bridge

Times Square

Madison Square

Broadway

Washington Square

Greenwich Village

Wall Street

Castle Garden

Trinity Church

They would not appear for another ten years.

Broadway at this time was one of New York's finest streets. It began at the spot where old Fort Amsterdam had stood until 1789.

Broadway cuts diagonally through the island of Manhattan and divides it into two triangles. Broadway crosses most of Manhattan's streets at one place or another.

Almost all the streets are straight as an arrow. They run at right angles and divide the city into rectangular blocks. The streets that run the length of Manhattan are called avenues, and the ones that run the width of the island are called streets. Most of them are numbered, for example Eighth Avenue or 42nd Street.

Only the streets at the lower tip of Manhattan have names. These are the oldest streets, and they do not fit into the pattern of straight, numbered streets and avenues.

This geometric grid plan of the city was worked out in 1811. New York's city hall was built around that same time. The street plan was one of the first things decided in the new city hall.

The grid plan is not special for New York City. It has been used in many other cities. The unusual part of New York's plan is that it is

Sidewalk merchants in Union Square.

so big. It laid out 193 streets without any disruption in the plan except for Central Park.

Some people call the streets of Manhattan an asphalt jungle. Green areas and trees are few and far between, except for the big Central Park. In a way, the city and its streets surround the people who live there.

This was not the intention when the city plan was worked out in 1811. At that time, they had no idea that Manhattan would be completely covered with buildings within only ninety years. The original planners thought that Harlem, for example, would remain a rural area for hundreds of years. They put in the top 75 streets on the city plan simply for the sake of being complete.

During the first half of the 1800's, the streets of New York were already in need of widening. The great influx of immigrants began to overpopulate some parts of the city. Traffic grew and needed more room.

A European visitor, Henrik Cavling, described Broadway in 1897: "Up and down the street, a row of cable cars runs on two tracks, one car after the other. They are pulled along by underground cables, not by horses. These cable cars sound their warnings with violent bell ringing. But because the bells are ringing all the time, day and night, the only impression is that all kinds of accidents are happening to music instead of in silence."

These cable cars did not destroy the environment of the city streets as much as the elevated railway did. Broadway and the elegant Fifth Avenue were not affected, but people on other streets and

Elevated railway over Battery Park near Castle Garden, which can be seen in the background.

avenues had to live with the "elevated" for many years.

The trains rode on rails that were raised above the street on a skeleton of steel. At third story level, the elevated rumbled along, crowded in between the rows of houses, as far as the eye could see.

The first elevated railways in New York were built in the 1870's as an experiment. By 1890, a network of elevated railways covered the lower part of Manhattan up to Central Park.

The elevated railways were not built without protest. Many people asserted that they ruined the environment of the city. The scenic Battery Park near Castle Garden was cut through by a network of elevated railways. But the system came to stay.

The last elevated railways on Manhattan were torn down after World War II. In other parts of New York—Brooklyn and the Bronx—they still exist.

Land Prices

Landowners along the wide avenues hoped to make money when the elevated railway project came into their part of the city. As the elevated was built further and further north, the prices of land and buildings rose. Faster transportation increased the value of property.

But speculation did not always pay.

In Harlem, hundreds of landowners went bankrupt around

27

1900 because construction of the elevated was delayed. They had paid high prices for their real estate. They expected prices to rise even higher when the elevated came to Harlem, but it did not come soon enough for many of them. They had to sell their property at a loss.

Opponents of the elevated wanted subways instead. They had some success. New York's first subway was built in 1904.

Elevated railway station on the Manhattan end of the Brooklyn Bridge, offering a fine view of New York in 1900.

The elevated tracks on Manhattan were torn down in the 1950's.

Immigrant Ghettos

The Lower East Side Around 1890

Thousands of immigrants settled in an area behind the high buildings and elegant stores of Broadway. This area was called the Lower East Side. It was one of the worst slums in America.

The street scene changed in this part of Manhattan. The elevated did not really run through this part of town. Neither did the horse drawn omnibuses nor the cable cars. They could not push their way through these narrow streets, filled with people.

Everything was dirty in the Lower East Side. The buildings were four to six story tenements in bad condition. Most of them had been built after 1870 to house large numbers of immigrants.

During the day, the streets hummed with the shouts of children and adults and with the cries of peddlers, standing by their pushcarts in the street and selling cabbage, fruit, flowers, or many other goods.

Jacob A. Riis photo of a street in the Lower East Side, 1890.

At night, people seemed to be sleeping in all kinds of odd places. Some slept in shacks and alleys or on the steps of buildings. These were the people who could not even afford the nickel it cost to sleep in a flophouse. Many of them were children who had no family.

The Lower East Side was over-populated. In the late 1800's, many of the people who lived there were Italians, Jews and other immigrants from eastern and southern Europe. Today, many of them are Puerto Ricans, other Hispanics and West Indians.

In the late 1800's, immigrants came to America without any knowledge of the terrible living conditions that would meet them. They had to be satisfied with any roof over their heads. There was no way for them to go back home, and no way for them to complain and be heard.

The slum landlords did not complain. They made a lot of money by crowding people into unsafe, filthy, rundown buildings.

Jacob A. Riis photo of Mulberry Street around 1900.

Around 1900, the authorities succeeded in cleaning up the worst slum areas.

The Lower East Side had to get along as best it could. The police did not bother the slum landlords. They had their hands full trying to prevent violence in the streets. Robbery and murder were daily events in the immigrant slums of the Lower East Side.

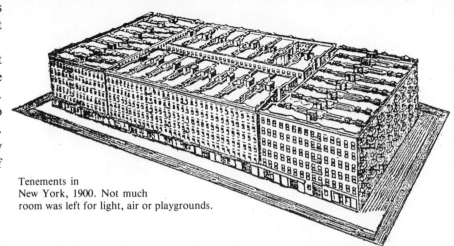

Tenements in New York, 1900. Not much room was left for light, air or playgrounds.

Tenements

Most tenement houses were built to cover about 90% of the lot. There was an open space at the back of the lot to serve as an air shaft for the rear apartments. It also let in a little light.

A typical tenement house around 1870 was built on a lot about 25 feet wide and 100 feet deep. These tenements were still in use around 1900. They generally had four apartments for four large families on each story. They were usually five stories high. This meant that there were 20 apartments and 100 to 150 people—sometimes more—living in a single building.

The tenements had been built in the cheapest possible way. They seldom had indoor bathrooms.

In 1894, the New York housing commission investigated bathing facilities for the 255,000 people who were living in the Lower East Side area. They found that only 306 of these people could take a bath in the building where they lived. In one case, 1,321 *families* had to share one single bathtub, according to the commission report.

Conditions inside the apartments were absolutely terrible in many cases. The rooms were small and damp. Walls were sometimes papered with old newspapers to cover the worst cracks and holes.

The journalist, Jacob A. Riis, in his book, *Out of Mulberry Street* (1898), gave this impression of an immigrant apartment in the Lower East Side: "The room is black with smoke and dirt. In the middle of the floor oozes an oil-stove that serves at once to take the raw edge off the cold and to cook meals by.

Half the window-panes are broken, and the holes stuffed with rags. The sleeve of an old coat hangs out of one, and beats drearily upon the sash when the wind sweeps over the fence and rattles the rotten shutters. The family's wash, clammy and gray, hangs on a clothes-line stretched across the room."

Sweatshops

Many immigrants lived the rest of their lives in these miserable apartments.

Families were taken advantage of by clever manufacturers and middlemen. They were put to work at home, earning only enough to pay their rent and buy their daily bread.

The little rooms became workshops as well as homes. Tools and

31

Immigrant home, 1911.

hemming trousers and dresses. Some sewed leather purses together. Others made belts, embroidered handkerchiefs, or sewed on buttons.

Some rolled cigars. Making 4,000 cigars a week gave an income of around $16.

These factory apartments were called "sweatshops." The middleman was called a "sweater." He came around every week and paid for the family's work. The goods they made were sold in shops on Broadway. Sometimes they went on to factories to be finished.

In 1895, the *New York Times* reported that 13,000 sweatshop tailors had stopped work and established a strike headquarters. They demanded agreements with the middlemen, so that only professionally trained tailors could work in the sweatshops. They also wanted higher pay and shorter hours—they demanded a 59 hour work week.

Labor unions found good conditions for growth in the working class neighborhoods of New York.

Sticking Together

But improvements were slow in coming. The Lower East Side was still a slum in the early 1900's.

materials littered the rooms, together with the family wash, the furniture, and all the members of the family themselves.

Despite the clutter, many immigrants liked to work this way. The family could stay together during their working day.

In the slums of the Lower East Side, recent immigrants to America are still working this way today. The pay is still very low, as it was in the early 1900's.

Thousands of immigrant families labored in their homes or in small basement rooms, sewing blouses or

32

Jacob A. Riis photo of a tailor's workshop, Lower East Side, around 1888

Danish immigrant tailors at work in New York.

Jacob A. Riis, Immigrant Journalist

Jacob A. Riis was the son of a school teacher in the small town of Ribe, Denmark.

Even as a child, he once shocked the town of Ribe by buying some strong soap and using it to clean the steps of the poor house.

As a young man, he learned the trade of cabinetmaker. At the age of 21, he emigrated to America to try his luck. That was in 1870. Things did not go so well at first.

One day, however, he managed to get a job in a news bureau. That was the beginning of his career in journalism—and it meant that the poor immigrants were soon to find their spokesman.

Jacob A. Riis soon showed great ability as a reporter. He made the Lower East Side his specialty. His reports became front page news. By the end of the 1880's, he began taking photographs to illustrate his stories. At that time, they could not print photographs in a newspaper. The technique had not yet been invented. So the newspapers had artists who could draw newspaper illustrations from the photographs.

Jacob A. Riis developed a social awareness. He spoke for the cause of the poor in his articles and pictures. But many columns of

As the rest of Manhattan changed, it became more difficult for the immigrant families to survive. Many small industries were forced to move out and relocate in northern Manhattan.

The immigrants who lived on the Lower East Side had to travel up to northern Manhattan every day in order to work in the factories. But they would not move.

Immigrants considered their community life to be more important than living close to work. They wanted to live together with people who spoke their own language. Often the residents of a tenement had come from the same village in Europe. Old friends and neighbors were all around in the tenement district.

Jacob A. Riis wrote that 67,000 of the 140,000 Italians who came to New York in 1891 settled in the Mulberry Street area or in the Italian section of Harlem. Whole sections of New York City became dominated by a single ethnic group.

The more wealthy New Yorkers who used to live in the streets near Broadway began to move out. They did not care to live so close to the poor immigrants. They moved to new apartments in quieter neighborhoods in Greenwich Village or along Central Park.

Jacob A. Riis.

newspaper stories had to be printed before the politicians in city hall began to show any interest in the people of the slums, just a few hundred yards down the street from city hall.

Dangerous Trips

Riis' work among the poor of New York put him in danger many times. One day, a man with a knife attacked him. Another time, he barely avoided being hit by a flying bottle when he found himself in the middle of a barroom brawl.

Sometimes people threw rocks and other things at him when he took their pictures.

No wonder the people of the slums were skeptical when Riis showed up with his equipment. The flash bulb had not yet been invented. Riis had to use flash powder to light up the dark places he photographed.

He purchased his flash powder in cartridges that were shot off in a revolver. With these in hand, he and his four or five assistants did not need police protection on their nightly picture taking adventures. The sight of five or six men, pushing their way into a house at night, armed with big pistols, was not something that inspired confidence, even if they were speaking in a reassuring way.

35

Results

Political results finally occurred when Riis put all of his material into a book in 1890. The book was called *How the Other Half Lives.* It caused a sensation.

A new welfare law was one result. The worst areas of the slums were cleaned out. A large area of old tenements was razed to the ground and replaced by a park.

Riis considered this park to be his greatest accomplishment. He was disappointed when the park was named for Columbus and not for Riis. He felt that he had brought the park into existence.

With that thought on his mind, he walked down one sunny day to see the park. Children were playing in one corner. Riis, who loved children, walked across "his" lawn to watch them. He had not gone far before he was stopped by a policeman. For once, Riis' way with words did not help. After a heated exchange, he was taken by the collar and thrown out of Columbus Park.

You were not allowed to walk on the grass.

Old Mrs. Benoit at work in her room on the Lower East Side.

Crowded bedroom in a flophouse

Jacob A. Riis Photographs.

This man slept here for four years, according to Riis.

Children of the streets have found a warm place to sleep in cold weather.

Immigrant street musicians.

City Politics

Political Corruption

The poverty of the New York slums was in dramatic contrast to the great wealth in other parts of the city. New York's tremendous rate of development meant that the problems of the poor had to wait. All attention was drawn to the reckless battle of the financial czars for power and money.

This battle was waged on the stock exchange and in the banks. The battle was also felt at city hall.

Here the prizes were great city contracts for the construction of streets, bridges and buildings. There was fierce competition for these contracts. The battle was waged with bribery and other forms of corruption.

Political corruption grew by leaps and bounds in New York during the 1800's. One of the centers of corruption came to be the notorious Tammany Hall organization.

This was a political organization that gained influence in city politics. Tammany Hall put up candidates for the offices of mayor and city council. They were able to get plenty of economic support during the campaigns. This support came from the rich and powerful members of the organization.

Nobody in the Tammany organization hesitated to give money to a candidate who was backed by Tammany Hall. They knew that if

New York Gold Exchange, 1875.

their candidate won, the money would come back with interest.

It would be paid back in the form of city contracts for materials and supplies. These contracts were given to people who had supported the successful candidates during the campaign. Or it might be in the form of lucrative building contracts from city hall. These contracts were only awarded to those who had good political contacts with city government.

Exposing Corruption

During the summer of 1871, bribery of public officials was stopped for a time in New York.

The *New York Times* ran a sensational, three-week series of stories exposing the unparalleled corruption in New York city government. The climax of the series was the July 29 issue of the newspaper, which was devoted completely to stories about the scandal.

The citizens of New York could now read about how they had been duped for more than ten years.

An audit of the city books showed that crooked businessmen had earned tremendous fortunes on city contracts. They had known somebody who made certain that their bills would be paid without question.

Political demonstration outside Tammany Hall in New York, 1844.

A carpet dealer, for example, had been paid $175,000 for laying carpet in some new city offices. Another had provided thermometers to the same offices at a cost to the city of $7,500.

The scandal had many aspects. One of the worst was in city bonds. 39

William Marcy Tweed.

Voters imprisoned for election fraud in New York, 1876.

Manhattan was consolidated with four neighboring communities of Brooklyn, Queens, the island of Richmond (Staten Island), and the Bronx.

This consolidation had been under consideration for a long time.

Andrew Haswell Green had won great popularity in New York around 1850 because of his planning of Central Park. Then he became an early spokesman for consolidation. That cost him much of his popularity.

Local patriotism was still strong in the two largest communities, New York and Brooklyn. Most people could not accept Green's

For a number of years, the city had sold bonds without any security.

This had all taken place under the leadership of William Marcy Tweed, called Boss Tweed.

These disclosures meant that a large number of banks all over America had to stop loans to New York City. The bonds of New York City were no longer sold on the major international stock exchanges.

It was a hard blow to the city of New York. Both politics and city finances had to be cleaned up. The city debt had grown in just four years from $30 million to $90 million.

The citizens of New York never learned how much they had really lost. Some estimates were around $50 million. Others were as high as $200 million.

Boss Tweed never revealed anything. He died in prison at the age of 55 in 1878.

The Great Consolidation

In 1898, the opportunities for fraud in New York City finances were decreased by a massive reorganization of city government. Until that time, the city of New York had not reached beyond the island of Manhattan. Now

The five boroughs of New York City.

Manhattan

Bronx

Queens

Brooklyn

Richmond

Central Park around 1875.

ideas of consolidation. Green maintained that the need for more bridges and elevated railways across the East River could not be met without consolidation.

Consolidation had to wait quite a while. Time proved Green to be right. The problems of New York's growth could only be solved through consolidation and cooperation.

New Year's Eve, 1897, was the date finally set for consolidation.

New York was again decorated for a celebration. And again it rained.

The rain poured down on people in the streets all evening long. Then the rain turned to snow. The city was filled with sleet and slush.

But people did not go home. It was New Year's Eve. Fireworks and rockets were shot off along the East River. At precisely midnight, all the church bells in the city rang. Choirs began singing throughout

the city. The celebration seemed to go without end.

The next day, the *New York Times* reported that the sun had risen over the largest metropolitan experiment in the world. "The end of the old New York and the beginning of the greater city were marked last night by perhaps the biggest, noisiest and most hilarious New Year's Eve celebration that Manhattan Island has ever known."

Empire State Building, 102 stories high, dominating the Manhattan skyline. It was built in 1931 and was the tallest building in the world for 40 years.

Brooklyn Bridge

Building the Bridge

The French architect, Le Corbusier, wrote in his book, *When the Cathedrals Were White,* "A considerable part of New York is nothing more than a provisional city. A city which will be replaced by another city."

This is the way it had been since the city began to expand in the early 1800's. New York was constantly being rebuilt.

The city's talent for trade brought large amounts of money to Manhattan. Many companies established head offices or branches in the city. These head offices and branches often became larger and more elegant than in other cities.

All this activity provided work for the many immigrants. Great projects like the building of the Empire State Building in 1931, and the construction of bridges across the river around Manhattan, provided many jobs.

In the years between 1869 and 1883, the Brooklyn Bridge was New York's largest place of employment.

Brooklyn Bridge under construction around 1881.

The German born engineer, John A. Roebling, designed the bridge, and his son, Washington A. Roebling, helped to build it.

The construction of the Brooklyn Bridge was followed by the citizens of New York with great interest. A speech made a few days after construction began shows how much New Yorkers expected of the bridge: "Now the bridge will finally be built. It will arouse our pride and our thankfulness. When it is finally finished, it will symbolize the greatness of our era. It will become a Mecca attracting visitors from afar. Babylon had its hanging gardens, Nineveh its towers, Rome the Colosseum. New York will have this grand monument to progress."

The same day, the chief engineer, John A. Roebling, suffered an injury in an accident. This led to delay of the whole immense project.

Problems

The accident happened on Monday, June 28, 1869. While inspecting the excavations for the foundations of the bearing cables,

John A. Roebling.

and dramatic than anyone had anticipated.

Twenty workers were killed during the fourteen years of construction. Accidents—and cost overruns that constantly threatened disaster—gradually weakened Roebling's hold on the project. From the middle of the 1870's and on, he was so exhausted that he did not have the strength to go out to the construction site.

Sick and broken, he used a telescope to follow the construction from his home in Brooklyn, a few hundred yards from the bridge. His second in command had to come to Roebling's apartment every morning to get orders.

Caissons

The bridge towers rested on two immense caissons. They were built of wood and iron, then dug into the river bottom in the years 1870-1871. They were 170 feet long, 100 feet wide, and 15 feet high. The caissons were five feet thick on top, but the sides were thinner and there was no bottom. They were built to support themselves on the river bottom.

After they had been set in place and sunk to the bottom, the caissons were filled with compressed air. The air pressure gave

Roebling stumbled over a wire. He fell in such a way that the tip of one toe was clipped off.

But Roebling was tough. He refused medical attention, wrapped up the toe himself, and limped down into the excavation. Unfortunately, the wound was not cleaned properly. Infection set in and spread to the foot and leg. Three weeks later, he was dead.

His son, Washington A. Roebling, was then appointed as his father's successor. The city had no choice: the bridge could wait no longer. The son had taken part in all of his father's planning.

Washington A. Roebling became a popular figure in the press during the first years of construction. But before long, problems occurred that were more serious

44

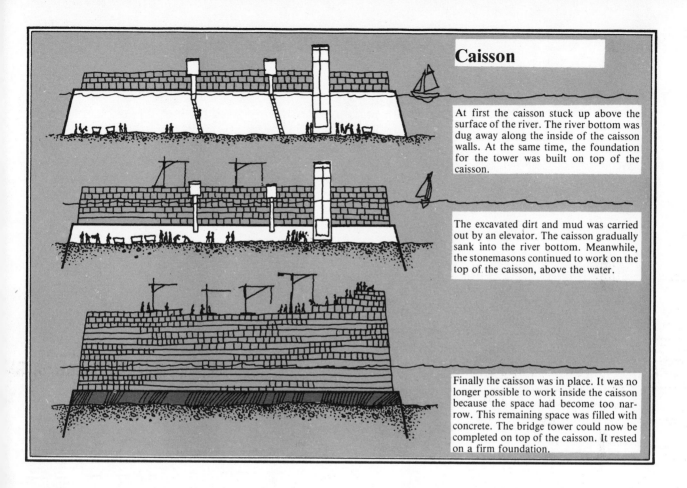

Caisson

At first the caisson stuck up above the surface of the river. The river bottom was dug away along the inside of the caisson walls. At the same time, the foundation for the tower was built on top of the caisson.

The excavated dirt and mud was carried out by an elevator. The caisson gradually sank into the river bottom. Meanwhile, the stonemasons continued to work on the top of the caisson, above the water.

Finally the caisson was in place. It was no longer possible to work inside the caisson because the space had become too narrow. This remaining space was filled with concrete. The bridge tower could now be completed on top of the caisson. It rested on a firm foundation.

added support to the top. The foundations of the two bridge towers were built of huge stones on top of the caissons. At the same time, the sides of the caissons were dug into the river bottom. The weight of the rising foundations pushed them down.

The high air pressure inside the caissons was maintained by a system of pumps. The workers came in and out through an airtight hatch. It was like a series of barrels rising above the caisson. There were several compartments, so that the air did not escape when the doors were opened, one at a time. This series of hatches was always above the water level. Access to the caisson was made easier by the fact that it was close to the shore.

When the work inside the caisson was finished, the remaining space was filled with concrete. David McCullough describes all of this in his book, *The Great Bridge* (1972).

45

On the Job

The first caisson was put into position on the Brooklyn end of the bridge. Three shifts of men worked at digging out the mud, rocks and dirt along the inside walls of the caisson.

There could be 112 workers in the caisson at one time. But the space was crowded and the air was bad. Most of them quit after a few days on the job. Every third worker quit after only a week on the river bottom. New men had to be hired all the time. Almost 2,500 workers took part in the excavation of the caisson on the Brooklyn side.

The compressed air in the caisson was hard to take. The deeper down the caisson went, the higher the air pressure had to be. Many men got sick on the job. Some fainted when they came up to fresh air.

Towards the end, conditions in the caisson were so bad that the wages were raised from $2 to $2.25 a day, just to keep the work going.

The higher wages made it possible to entice the poorest immigrant workers to go down into the caisson. They were mostly Italians, Irish and Germans.

The wages added up to $13.50 a week if you could last a whole week. In the sweatshops of the Lower East Side, a whole family

1

2

3

46

Building the Brooklyn Bridge

1. The foundation rises on top of the caisson, which has not yet been dug very far into the river bottom.
2. Breaking up a rock underneath the caisson wall.
3. On the way into the caisson, a series of airlocks helped to prevent a loss of the high pressure inside the caisson.
4. The ladder up to the airlock passage.
5. Installing the bearing cables.
6. Rigging the bearing cables.

47

could earn no more than $16 a week. In comparison, a famous and talented journalist like Jacob A. Riis earned only $23 a week in 1889.

Under the River

In addition to the high air pressure, there were other things that made it rough to work in the caissons.

There was almost no fresh air down there. The cramped working space had a terrible odor. At the same time, water kept seeping in. The caisson was always full of deep mud.

One thing about the caisson, however, was the best in the world. That one thing was the toilet. One of Roebling's official reports described it as a pneumatic water toilet. It was flushed by compressed air.

The toilet was in one corner of the caisson. It was a wooden box with a lid. A long pipe went up and out through the top of the caisson. To flush it, you simply opened a valve in this pipe. The high air pressure inside the caisson quickly flushed out the toilet into the river.

Fire in the Caisson

It was 7:00 a.m. on Friday, December 2, 1870. People were on their way to work all over New York. The rumor of tragedy spread rapidly in the train stations and at omnibus stops. The caisson was burning. Some said that many workers had been killed.

Crowds of people lined the ferry docks between Manhattan and Brooklyn. The harbor fire boats were spraying water on the caisson. Nothing more could be seen.

Inside the caisson, workers were frantic at first. The fire was burning deep inside the layer of beams over their heads. There was only a short period of panic among the 80 workers who were in the caisson when the fire broke out. Contrary to rumor, no one had been killed. But they all knew that if the fire was not put out quickly, the caisson could collapse. Then they would all be killed.

On top of the caisson, 28,000 tons of stone blocks formed the foundation of the tower.

Washington Roebling had been called to the scene immediately. He worked frantically with his men to reach the fire and put it out. Some suggested that the caisson should be flooded to douse the fire. Roebling said no, it would take hours for the water to soak into the twelve-inch beams of the ceiling. Furthermore, the whole caisson might tip if they tried to flood it.

The compressed air fed the fire. The flames ate through the beams. Layer after layer was destroyed. Roebling and his men could not stop the fire. The caisson had to be filled with water after all. Water was pumped through the airlock by the harbor fire boats. They used 38 hoses. Seven hours later, the caisson was filled and the fire was almost out.

Two days later, workers began to clean up. Ruined beams had to be replaced. Some places were patched with cement. This work took about four months.

This fire caused a serious delay that did not fit very well into the fast pace of life in New York City. Many newspaper editorials were written on the subject.

How could such a fire break out? One newspaper, *The World,* guessed sabotage. This was disputed by other newspapers. The cause of the fire was never determined. Soon the newspapers found other things to write about.

The construction of the two immense towers on top of the caissons took place in full view of the public. This work was followed with much more interest than the mysterious digging in the caissons on the bottom of the river.

go out on the bridge in order to admire the view. Suddenly a woman tripped and fell on the boardwalk. Nothing happened to her, but she was frightened and she screamed.

Her scream touched off a wave of terror on the whole bridge. "Now it's falling," somebody shouted.

Panic broke loose. Nobody could see what had happened. People rushed for land. At the bridge tower, all consideration for others was forgotten. There was a mad rush to get through the portal and down the ramp.

When the bridge was finally empty, bleeding and injured people lay all around the portal. Many of them had had their clothing almost ripped off in the turmoil.

The newspapers criticized the authorities for not having police stationed on the bridge. But the panic was never repeated.

People finally began to accept the fact that the world's longest suspension bridge in 1883 might just stay where it was.

The sidewalk of the Brooklyn Bridge was above the traffic lanes.

Panic

The bridge was dedicated in 1883. The towers rose some 280 feet above the surface of the river. It was a grand sight.

The proud dreams of New Yorkers seemed at last to have come true. But there were many who were skeptical. There had been too many accidents on this bridge already. Many people refused to believe that a suspension bridge could be held up by nothing but cables. They were afraid that it would crash down into the

The dedication of the made people even more One week later, their fe disasterous results.

It was on Memorial D About 20,000 people ha

The Brooklyn Bridge rose far above the low buildings of the Lower East Side of Manhattan.

The Millionaire's New York

Fifth Avenue

During the wave of immigration between 1860 and 1920, the population of New York grew rapidly. In 1860, there were 1.2 million people in the city. By 1920, there were 5.6 million.

Among other things, this brought about a tremendous building boom. The city changed all the time. Only one area of Manhattan remained free of overpopulation. This was the central part of Fifth Avenue.

The rich lived there. These were people who had acquired tremendous fortunes during the 1800's by building railroads, banking, engaging in trade, government contracting or manufacturing. There were people like Cornelius Vanderbilt, who left an estate of $105 million. When his son, William Vanderbilt, died eight years later, the fortune had grown to $200 million.

Millionaires considered Fifth Avenue a pleasant place to live, especially the part along Central Park. Their riding horses could be

aired in the park each afternoon. In the evening, they were close to the opera and theater—only a 15-minute carriage ride from Times Square.

The fact that the rich all lived close together led to an extravagant and flamboyant life style. For a full generation, jealousy and personal triumph alternated in the lives of the rich along Fifth Avenue, as they all strove to keep up with one another in the display of wealth.

These millionaires tried to outdo each other in the building of elaborate mansions, in furnishing them with the most expensive paintings and furniture, and in staging incredible entertainments.

Around 1880, the huge mansions stood side by side along Central Park. They were all built like palaces or castles out of the past, with many towers and spires. All the famous historical styles of Europe were represented. A mansion built like a medieval German castle might stand right next door to one like a columned palace of the Italian Renaissance.

Nothing is Timeless

The worst of it all was that most of these palaces on which such fantastic sums of money had been spent stood for only about 50 years. Then they were torn down and replaced by modern, expensive apartment buildings.

The great mansions simply cost too much to maintain. Some of them had huge banqueting halls and incredible numbers of rooms. One had no less than 150 rooms. After 1900, nobody wanted to live in a house like that anymore. Not

Easter Sunday on Fifth Avenue, 1906.

Cornelius Vanderbilt's grandson owned this mansion near Central Park. It was torn down in 1927.

Banqueting with the rich.

even the rich had such luxurious habits any longer.

The growing social consciousness of ordinary people was the thing that put an end to this luxury. The newspapers began to write critical stories about life on Fifth Avenue.

Soon it was no longer fashionable to throw parties where the guests were all dressed in priceless costumes centuries old, or parties where the banquet was served on horseback while servants rushed around, sweeping up the litter on the floor into little silver dustpans.

Things like that were now considered vulgar.

Life on Fifth Avenue became more private and discreet. The millionaires no longer wanted to attract attention.

Broken Dreams

Harlem By Night

The name of the Lafayette Theater shone in bright lights. It was a Saturday evening in 1920. People were lined up in front of the ticket counter. The show was a revue starring a number of Black entertainers and jazz musicians.

Some of the people in the line were Black. The Lafayette was one of the first theaters in New York to allow Blacks to sit where they wanted. In other places, Blacks had to sit in the last rows or in the balcony. Some theaters were reserved for whites only.

The theater was on the corner of Seventh Avenue and 131st Street. This was in the part of Harlem that first had Black residents.

The streets in this part of Harlem were lined with four and five story buildings. There were trees along the avenues and broad streets. The buildings were brown sandstone, just like many of the mansions on Fifth Avenue.

The buildings in Harlem were not very well maintained, and the sidewalks were cracked. But this could not be seen at night.

The lights shone in front of the many restaurants and nightclubs that had sprung up in Harlem in the years between 1912 and 1920. People came from all over New York to Harlem to have a good time. Music was everywhere, especially on Saturday nights. A jazz pianist was performing in one place, a blues singer in another, and in a third, a full orchestra with chorus and dancers.

When Duke Ellington came to Harlem for the first time in 1923 as a young man, he exclaimed, "The world's most glamorous atmosphere. Why, it is just like the Arabian Nights!"

From Rural Village to City Slum

All Black newcomers were impressed with New York. They saw great possibilities for progress in Harlem. They believed that they would be able to create a new kind of Black society in a place like this. They expected Harlem to become the Black capital of the world.

For a time, it was. A brilliant blossoming of African-American cultural activity called the Harlem Renaissance took place in the 1920's and 1930's. Famous black writers like W. E. B. DuBois, Langston Hughes and James Weldon Johnson contributed to the Harlem Renaissance.

But the dream was tarnished by much misery.

Harlem had been a peaceful and poor village community since the

Sam Wooding's orchestra was one of many that brought jazz to Harlem in the 1920's. In 1925, it became the first Black orchestra to tour Europe.

1700's. The inhabitants supported themselves by raising sheep and a few field crops.

Around 1870, big things began to happen.

One carriage after another rolled in from New York. Old farmhouses were bought and torn down. Lots were laid out and streets built. Apartment buildings began to shoot up all over.

Within a few years, the fields were crisscrossed with streets, all the way up to the northernmost end of Manhattan. Thirty years later, it was hard to find a vacant lot in Harlem. The few vacant lots that were left were tremendously expensive.

The development of Harlem was directed by the great captains of finance in New York. They had discovered Harlem when it was merged with New York City in the 1870's. This happened at the same time that three elevated railways were being constructed.

The captains of finance knew that houses and buildings increased in value as soon as the elevated railway was built near them. Therefore, they were convinced that building projects in Harlem would eventually lead to tremendous profits.

The "sweet life" in Harlem, 1927.

They built elegant apartments, not tenement houses. The apartments in Harlem were spacious and beautiful. They were built for prosperous middle class New Yorkers.

Economic Collapse
The boom of building speculation in Harlem was only partly suc-cessful. By 1900, some 100,000 tenants had been lured to Harlem by the impressive advertisements for these elegant new apartments. That was quite a few people, compared with the 91 families who lived there in 1820. But it was not enough. Far from it. Many apartments stood empty for years. It seemed that the real estate speculators had built too much too fast.

The speculators were not easily discouraged. They still figured that they could always sell the buildings at a profit. Everybody seemed to believe that all the apartments would be rented as soon as the streets were improved. By then, the subway would also be finished all the way down Manhattan from Harlem to the Brooklyn Bridge.

Speculators lived high on these hopes for many years. The apartment houses of Harlem were well built. They were handsome buildings. Harlem was an area of trees, green boulevards, and quiet. It was a good place to live.

The speculators had overlooked just one thing. Harlem was too far away.

For people who had to go to work in lower Manhattan every

Apartment houses arising among the farms and fields of Harlem around 1889.

57

day, Harlem was too far away, even if all three elevated railways were running. Moreover, there was no good place to shop in Harlem. And the entertainment was far away in Times Square.

More and more people began to realize that Harlem had been over-built. Not enough people wanted to live so far away from lower Manhattan. At least not the kind of people who could afford these luxurious apartments.

When the banks in 1904 suddenly stopped loans for the purchase of real estate in Harlem, the truth became crystal clear. The Harlem real estate market fell apart from one day to the next.

Within a few days, it became impossible to sell these expensive apartment buildings at almost any price. Nobody wanted to buy them any longer. And there was still a shortage of tenants in Harlem, so that many apartments stood vacant.

Then one day, somebody got the idea of renting to Blacks.

Policeman helps children across a Harlem street in 1899. The children are well dressed, and all of them are white. Blacks have not yet come to Harlem.

Blacks
Come to Harlem

New Tenants

It would not be true to say that Blacks were welcomed with open arms in Harlem. White New Yorkers were not tolerant of outsiders. Italian immigrants had felt this when they settled in the riverside areas near Harlem around 1890. "The smell from their awful dwellings disturbs their neighbors in respectable brownstone houses," wrote the *Harlem Local Reporter* in 1894.

Later, Jewish immigrants from eastern Europe were the target. They were more or less excluded from Harlem. "Keine Juden und keine Hunde," read a sign on a street corner. "No Jews and no dogs."

Two elderly Black women in Harlem, 1900.

Blacks began moving in around 1900. People were even more hostile to Blacks than to immigrants.

A Black realtor, Philip A. Payton, Jr., began to specialize in renting to Blacks. He came to be called the "Father of Colored Harlem."

White landlords went on the attack. They signed pledges that they would not rent to Blacks. They were afraid that the presence of Black tenants would drive down the value of their expensive apartment buildings.

But it did not work. Many of the owners were close to bankruptcy. They could not afford to have their apartment houses half empty. They had to find tenants or they would be forced to sell out at a loss. If they could not find white tenants, Black tenants would have to do.

New ways of making money in real estate soon came into use.

One of the most effective was to suggest that a "white" building was going to be rented to Blacks. That led the owner of the building next door to react. He might want to sell out. He would take almost any offer. His apartment building

New York City street.

could then be bought for a low price.

If that did not work, there were other methods. The speculator would rent out his apartment building to Blacks. Then prices on neighboring buildings fell automatically, and the speculator could buy them for a low price. Now he could rent out more apartments to Blacks and earn good profits because he had bought the buildings cheaply.

Harlem Changes

In 1893, a white publication, *Harlem Monthly Magazine,* had predicted that the center of style, wealth, culture and intelligence would soon be found in the illustrious, old city of Harlem.

The Blacks of Harlem took over this dream, reshaped it and gave it a new significance in the years after 1900. Their dream was the one that led to the Harlem Renaissance.

A Black author, James Weldon Johnson, wrote about the future of Harlem in *The New York Age* in 1920. He predicted that this splendid part of New York would soon be the world's largest Negro city.

By 1920, 60,000 Blacks had moved into Harlem. At the same time, moving vans emptied one white apartment after the other. Real estate changed hands as luxurious apartment buildings were sold out at low prices. Harlem had once had New York's most expensive real estate market. Now it became the cheapest.

Smaller industrial plants began to move into the area. Thousands of poorly educated, low wage workers lived in Harlem. There was no labor shortage there.

Black hopes sank rapidly, even though Harlem tried to keep up a good front. The Chamber of Commerce arranged street carnivals and parades. They would show the people of New York that there was life in Harlem.

This helped a little, but not much.

Among the swelling Black population, unemployment grew, and with unemployment, hopelessness. Coupled with the tremendous cultural vitality of the Harlem Renaissance came the problems of a growing Black ghetto.

West Indians

More Blacks streamed into Harlem every day. By 1930, about 200,000 had settled there. The once elegant apartments were now run down and overcrowded. Harlem was slowly turning into a slum.

Blacks came to Harlem mainly from the South. They moved north looking for work. They also hoped to find more freedom in the north. For them, Harlem became a symbol of freedom.

Blacks from outside the United States came to Harlem. At that time, there was virtually no emigration from Africa. But large numbers of Blacks came from the islands of the Caribbean in the 1920's. Their culture and way of life was different from that of American Blacks. Many of them spoke Spanish instead of English.

The high hopes that Blacks brought to Harlem in the 1920's were battered by the depression of the 1930's and World War II in the 1940's. By the 1950's and 1960's, depression gave way to desperation.

The Harlem Renaissance came to an end. New centers of African-American culture arose in other parts of the land.

Castle Garden

Castle Garden and Ellis Island

The rest of New York was not very much affected by the movement of Blacks into Harlem. Immigrants from Europe usually settled along the rivers or on the Lower East Side. Many descendants of immigrants still live in these areas.

The great immigration is now past. Its two centers in New York have become historical sites. They commemorate the great waves of immigrants that came through the city in the years 1860-1920.

One site is the ruins of Castle Garden on Manhattan's southern tip. The other is Ellis Island in New York Bay.

Castle Garden is the oldest of the two. It functioned as the immigration station from 1855 until 1891. About eight million immigrants entered the United States through Castle Garden during that period.

It was finally closed because it was too small for the rising numbers of immigrants. A new immigration station was built on Ellis

Medical examination in Castle Garden.

Island. Large buildings covered the whole little island. The Ellis Island station was in use until 1954. By that time, immigration had fallen to such a low level that the station was closed.

The buildings still stand, but they are not used any more. They are administered as part of the museum of immigration on Statute of Liberty Island nearby.

Immigrants Arrive

Castle Garden was a massive, round building with walls over a yard thick. It had been built in 1807 as part of New York's defense system, but it had never really been used as a fort.

After standing unused for a while, Castle Garden was remodeled for use as a theater and exhibit hall. The Swedish opera singer, Jenny Lind, had her American debut there in 1850.

By 1855, the center of New York was moving further north. It became hard to get people to come to events way down at Castle

63

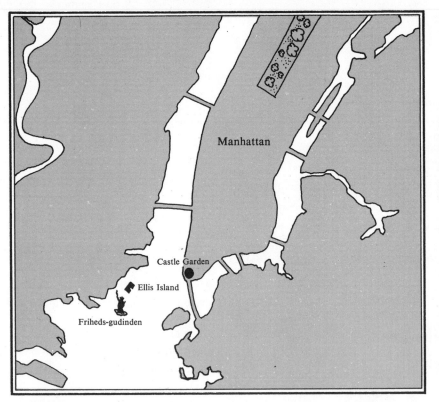

▲ Castle Garden around 1885.
◄ Ellis Island around 1925.

Garden. The old building was closed as a theater and taken over by the immigration authorities.

The stage was remodeled with desks for the registration of passengers from the immigrant ships. The lobby was changed into offices and examination rooms.

In March of 1871, *Harper's New Monthly Magazine* described a typical day in Castle Garden.

An ocean liner had arrived from Europe. It was the S/S Holland of Liverpool.

At the Desk

"The steerage passengers were being landed. It was a motley, interesting throng. Slowly, one by one, the new-comers passed the two officers whose duty it is to register every immigrant's name, birthplace, and destination.

"The officer in charge must be able to speak and understand nearly every language under the sun."

Sometimes the immigrants were suspicious and uncooperative.

"An old woman, on being asked her name, said that that was on her box, 'an' if we wanted to know, sure we could go and see.' "

At the ticket counter, there were other problems.

"A passenger (a Swede) desired to go to Farmington. But as there are no less than twenty-one cities and villages of that name in the United States, this address was hardly satisfactory. He was asked by the Danish clerk attached to the Railway Bureau what *state* that particular Farmington lay in; but this he could not tell."

"Finally he remembered some,ing about 'Da,' or 'Dada,' or 'Dakota;' and it was found to be 'Farmington, Dakota County, Minnesota,' a fact which was proved correct by letters which he afterward produced from his trunk."

It was not easy to be an immigration clerk at Castle Garden. But it was even worse to be an immigrant. They sometimes met a scorn reflected by the writer of the article in *Harper's Magazine* when he speaks of Swedes in terms of an ethnic stereotype.

"They are an excellent class of people, and form excellent and most desirable citizens, but cause a great deal of trouble on their arrival. In the first place they smell of a compound of leather, salt herring, onions, and perspiration, difficult to describe, but most apparent to the sense. Then they talk a language that none but a native Scandinavian can understand. They are, moreover...by nature rather suspecting and doubting."

This was typical of the way a whole ethnic group could be held

up to ridicule in one of America's most popular English language magazines in those days. Hostility towards immigrants was very strong in some circles.

Usually the immigrants had no reason to be suspicious of the officials at Castle Garden. They were there to help them on their way.

Only those immigrants who suffered from a contagious disease or had no money ran into trouble. They were put in quarantine on Ward's Island in the East River. They had to stay there until they regained their health or could scrape up some money from home or from friends and relatives in America.

After 1860, the whole of Ward's Island was used to relieve Castle Garden until the Ellis Island station was opened in 1892.

On Their Way

At the exit to Castle Garden, shouts were heard all day long. These were the agents and runners of cheap boarding houses, railway lines, porters and money changers, swindlers and cheats, trying to get the attention of the new arrivals.

Most of them were more or less crooked. An immigrant could be wiped out in a few minutes if he fell into their hands.

◄ Immigrants in Castle Garden.

The Museum of American Immigration on Statue of Liberty Island.

Even something as basic as renting a bed for the night could lead to problems. The immigrant usually had to check his baggage with the landlord. The rooms of the cheap hotels were so crowded that it was not possible to keep all the baggage by the bed.

When the immigrant was ready to move on, he came to pick up his belongings. Then he might be told that he had to pay storage costs and a handling fee. This might run to quite a bit of money.

Sometimes the immigrant did not have that much cash. So there was nothing to do but stay where he was until he had earned some money. In this way, dingy hotel keepers of the harbor area assured themselves of paying guests for long periods of time.

Life was hard. New York was no city for beginners.

Most immigrants had been warned before they left home. They knew that they had to take care of themselves once they were beyond the walls of Castle Garden. Nobody cared if they reached their goal or not. If they let someone cheat them out of money or belongings, that was their own problem. Then the trip beyond Castle Garden might be a short one. It would undoubtedly go by way of the Lower East Side slums.

New York was an impressive and inspiring city for those who had courage for the future. But it was also filled with pitfalls.

Much depended on the way the immigrants handled themselves from the first day of their arrival.

European refugees sailing into New York bay after World War II.

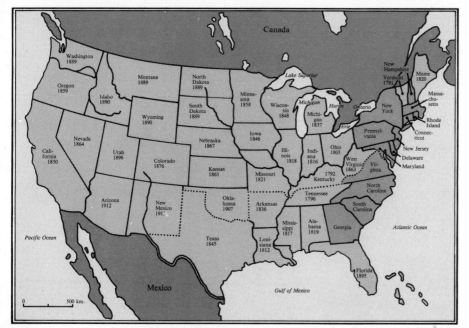

America 1914

The thirteen original states are shaded.

The dates indicate when the other states entered the union.

.....Border between North and South in 1861.

Since 1914, two states have joined the union: Alaska (1959) and Hawaii (1960).

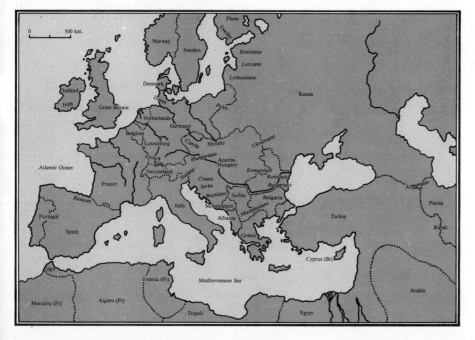

Europe 1914

The dotted lines indicate borders. *Italics* indicate national minorities.

Index

Picture Credits